FIND OUT ABOUT

ITALY

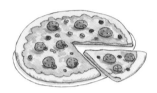

Where is Italy?

Italy is in southern Europe and stretches from the Alps to the Mediterranean Sea. It has sea on three sides (a peninsula), and is shaped like a long-legged boot with the island of Sicily at its toe.

This book tells you about Italy and its people. In Parts 1 and 2 you'll go on a journey around the country to learn how people live and work, and how to pronounce Italian words. In Part 3 there are lots of interesting facts about Italian history, famous men and women, and places to see. Then, in Part 4 you can learn some easy Italian to use in different situations you might meet during your vacation in one of Europe's largest and oldest countries.

You will meet the Rossi family, and especially their daughter Clara, age 11, and their son Marco, who is 9. They will help you to learn some Italian, and tell you about the things they enjoy doing.

Hi, I'm Clara. You'll meet me again with my brother on page 13.

2

How to say Italian words

In Italian every vowel and syllable is pronounced as you see it, and don't forget to roll the **r** – "*rrrr.*"

c is always soft when followed by **e** or **i** as in **cestino** (*cheh-stee-noh*) – basket, and **cipolla** (*chee-poll-lah*) – onion, but always hard when followed by **he** or **hi** as in **che** (*keh*) – what, and **chi** (*kee*) – who.

g is soft in **gelato** (*jeh-lah-toh*) – ice cream and **giro** (*jee-roh*) – trip, but hard in **ghepardo** (*ghe-pahr-doh*) – cheetah, and **ghiaccio** (*ghee-ahch-choh*) – ice.

gl after **i** as in **famiglia** – family is pronounced *fah-meel-yah*.

gn as in **gnocchi** – dumplings, the **g** is silent and pronounced *ny-ohk-kee*.

In Italian most words end in a vowel, e.g. **bagno** (*bahn-yoh*) – bathroom.

Talking to other people

There are four ways of saying "you" in Italian (familiar and polite, singular and plural). To a friend or family member you say **tu**, and **voi** for more than one. To someone you don't know very well you say **lei**, and **loro** for more than one.

gelato
jeh-lah-toh
ice cream

ghiaccio
ghee-ahch-choh
ice

4

a e i o u

a is pronounced like a short *ah*

e is a short *eh*

i is like *ee*

o is like *oh*

u is like *oo*

Masculine and feminine words

In Italian, all words are either masculine or feminine.

Il salotto – the living room – is masculine. **La** porta – the door – is feminine.

If there is more than one, "the" becomes **i** for masculine words and **le** for feminine words, e.g. **i** salotti – the living rooms – and **le** porte – the doors.

Accents

Accents on vowels are used for emphasis.

è is said with closed mouth.

é with open mouth.

à, **ì**, **ò** and **ù** are all open.

Vowels

Try saying **aiuole** (*ah-ee-oo-oh-leh*) – flowerbeds.

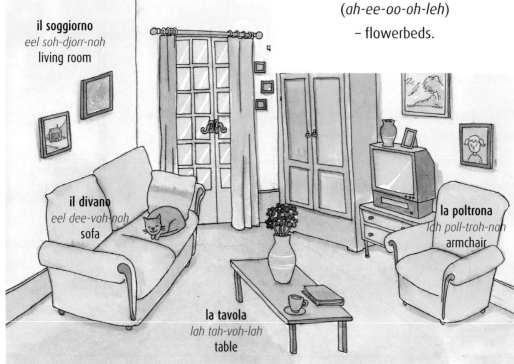

il soggiorno
eel soh-djorr-noh
living room

il divano
eel dee-vah-noh
sofa

la poltrona
lah poll-troh-noh
armchair

la tavola
lah tah-voh-lah
table

After a vowel or an "s" followed by a consonant, "i" becomes "gli."

Introduction

Find out what Italian people do in their spare time.

Did you know?

👍 The highest point in Italy is Mont Blanc de Courmayeur at 15,580 feet (4,748 m).

👍 Turin is the second city in Italy to host the winter Olympics. The first was Cortina d'Ampezzo, where the games were held in 1956.

👍 Italy became a nation-state under King Victor Emmanuel II in 1861, when the city-states of the peninsula and the islands of Sardinia and Sicily were united.

👍 There are 4,723 miles (7,600 km) of coastline, 12,000 miles (19,312 km) of railroad tracks and 298,065 miles (479,688 km) of roads in Italy.

👍 Two thirds of the UNESCO historical artistic heritage is in Italy.

👍 The longest river in Italy is the Po, which flows from near Turin in the northwest to the Adriatic sea.

👍 There are 58 million people in Italy and about 20% of the population is over 65.

👍 Italy is the fourth-most popular tourist destination in the world, with over 40 million visitors a year.

👍 Italy became a republic in 1946 and the design for the national flag was inspired by the French.

👍 Vatican City, an independent city-state within Rome, is home to the Pope and is protected by the Swiss Guards.

A trip around Italy

The capital of Italy is Rome, and the country consists of 20 regions and 95 provinces. Each region has its own customs, way of life, and food.

Italian is the main language, but each region has its own dialect or, in the case of Sardinia, its own language. In the Alpine region, various languages, including Friulian and Ladin, are spoken.

Most Italians are bilingual. That means that they speak both Italian and their regional dialect. Many Italians, even young people, continue to speak dialect at home and with their friends, rather than Italian.

Italian as a spoken language is based on the Tuscan dialect in which Dante Alighieri wrote *The Divine Comedy* in the Middle Ages.

The inhabitants of Siena and the surrounding area of Tuscany are considered to have the best Italian accent. People who live on the French or Swiss and Austrian borders of Italy speak heavily-accented Italian, and often speak French and German too.

il gondoliere
eel gon-doh-lee-ay reh
gondolier

la suora
lah soo oh-rah
nun

il contadino
eel kohn-tah-dee-noh
peasant farmer

l'impiegata
leem pee-eh-gah-tah
office worker

Italian dialects contain French, Spanish, German, and Arabic words.

Italy has a huge highway system and train network. Italian trains are very inexpensive and prices depend on the type of train you take. The most expensive is the bullet-shaped Eurostar (compulsory to book seats in advance). Despite what some people think, Italian trains are usually reliable.

Edicola

Go to *www.trenitalia.it* to find out more about Italian trains, destinations, and timetables. You can buy a comprehensive guide to train services called **l'orario dei treni** (*loh rah-ree-oh day-treh-nee*) at a newsstand (**l'edicola** *leh-dee-koh-lah*) to plan your trips in advance.

A highway is called an **autostrada** (*ow-toh-strah-dah*) and you must pay a toll at the **pedaggio** (*peh-dah-djoh*) to use it. The prices vary according to size of vehicle and even what highway you are on. Italians love driving, especially fast, and some drivers can be rather aggressive, so visitors will need to be careful on all Italian roads.

 Some Italian highways are amazing feats of engineering cutting through vast mountain ranges.

It is very easy to travel around Italy by car, train, or plane. There are small airports operating in most Italian cities. The month of August is the main Italian vacation season, so seaside resorts are very crowded. You may want to choose between visiting Northern or Southern Italy. The North is much more industrialized, and most resorts are very commercialized and regimented. Many beaches are private (run by hotels or restaurants) and the few public beaches are called **spiaggia libera** (*spee-ah-djah lee-beh-rah* free beach). The beaches in the South are more spacious and less spoiled, and the way of life is much more traditional than in the more progressive North.

The Pantheon, Rome

The Rialto Bridge, Venice

Italy has many important seaports including Genova (Genoa), Livorno (Leghorn), Civita Vecchia (near Rome). You can sail to the islands of Sardinia, Sicily, and Corsica, and even to Spain and the Canary Islands (from Genoa). From Ancona you can get a ferry to Greece and former Yugoslavia.

7

Low-cost airlines fly to many destinations in Italy. ☞

Rome and the big cities

Rome (Roma) is one of the most famous cities in the world. It was the heart of the Roman Empire and is home to the Pope in Vatican City, a separate state inside Rome.

St. Peter's Square

Rome has been the capital of a united Italy since 1871 and is Italy's largest city. It stands on the River Tiber in central Italy. The population is over 2.5 million.

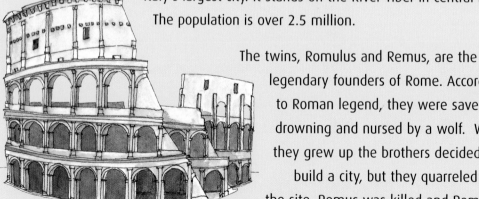

The Colosseum

The twins, Romulus and Remus, are the legendary founders of Rome. According to Roman legend, they were saved from drowning and nursed by a wolf. When they grew up the brothers decided to build a city, but they quarreled over the site. Remus was killed and Romulus became the city's sole ruler.

8

You can find out more on web sites like <u>www.romeguide.it</u> and <u>www.romaturismo.it</u>

The famous Spanish Steps are found in the **Piazza di Spagna** (Spanish Square). They were built in the 18th century, and lead to the 15th-century church of the Trinità dei Monti.

The Spanish Steps

Florence (Firenze) is the capital of Tuscany; it is in central Italy on the River Arno, below the Apennine mountains. Florence stands on the site of an Etruscan settlement that is well over 2,000 years old. The city is famous for its Gothic and Renaissance buildings, its rich art galleries, and its museums. It is also an important commercial, transport, and manufacturing center.

Santa Croce, Florence

The Ponte Vecchio over the River Arno, Florence

9

Put "Florence, Italy" into your search engine to find out more about this beautiful city.

Venice (Venezia) is a seaport in northeast Italy covering 120 islands formed by 177 canals on the edge of the Adriatic Sea. It was once a great naval and commercial power. A rail and road causeway connects Venice with the mainland. Long sandbars (barrier beaches) serve as protection against the sea. The islands forming the city are connected by

Grand Canal, Venice

about 400 bridges. No cars are permitted in the old city. In olden times, the most common means of transport was the **gondola** (*gon-doh-lah*), a flat-bottomed boat with a single oar. Today, gondolas are used mainly by tourists.

Milan (Milano) is in Lombardy in northern Italy. It is the second-largest Italian city and is a leading commercial, financial, and manufacturing center, having a major influence on the arts and fashion. The world's most famous opera house, La Scala, is in Milan. The world's leading opera singers and conductors perform here. The audience is notoriously critical and can make or break any performer.

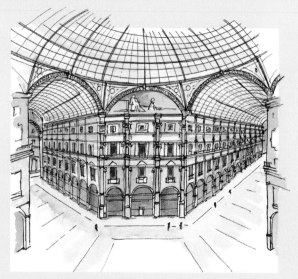

Shopping at the Galleria Vittorio Emanuele, Milan

10

Check out "La Scala" web site at: www.teatroallascala.org

The Bay of Naples

Naples (Napoli) is in Campania, southern Italy. It is an important seaport, below a range of hills bordering the Bay of Naples. Vesuvius, an active volcano towering over Naples, destroyed the two nearby Roman cities of Pompeii and Herculaneum in 79 A.D. Herculaneum is about 5 miles (8 km) east of Naples. Both cities were buried by many feet of lava, ash, and mud.

Turin (Torino) is in Piedmont, northwest Italy. It is the home of Fiat cars, and a major manufacturing center for leather and rubber items, clothing, and plastics. It is famous for the Turin Shroud (of Christ) although that has now been proved to be a fake.

Fiat is Italy's leading car manufacturer. The Agnelli family has been its owners since 1901. In recent times there have been economic problems, but their first profit in five years was recorded in 2005.

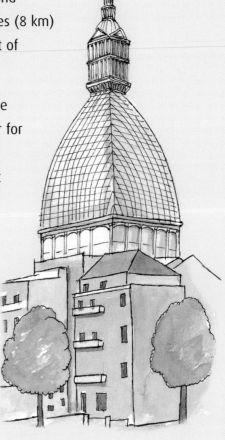

The Mole,
Turin

11

The *Mole Antonelliana* was named after its architect, Alessandro Antonelli.

Sports

The Italians are enthusiastic about sports. Soccer is a great passion. Italy beat France to win the 2006 World Cup.

Rugby is also played in most parts of the country. It's a game played with hands and feet, a little like American football. The U.S. takes part in the Rugby World Cup, a tournament held every four years.

Cycling is the most popular sport and most country roads (even the steepest) are full of colorful

Rugby boots

cycling enthusiasts. Italians follow the Tour de France bicycle race avidly. The first Italian to win this prestigious event was Ottavio Bottecchia in both 1924 and 1925.

Cycling

Cars and motor sports are very important to the Italians. The most famous event is the race at Monza where Formula 1 teams compete as part of the Grand Prix. The best Italian team is Ferrari which has drivers such as Michael Schumacher and Felipe Massa.

Ferrari

12

☞ At **www.letour.fr** find the highest placed Italian cyclist in the Tour de France in 2006.

Life in Italy

Learn useful words and phrases that will help you when you visit Italy.

Did you Know?

👍 The average Italian consumes 26 gallons (98 l) of wine a year.

👍 Pizza was invented by the cook Vincenzo Corrado in 1775 in Naples.

👍 Italy has more hotel rooms than any other European country.

👍 The famous Italian opera singer, Luciano Pavarotti, used to be a goalkeeper for his local soccer team, Modena.

👍 Gondolas in Venice are black (unless they are owned by a high official), because of a law passed in 1562 to prevent people from wasting money on paint and decorations.

👍 Each Italian consumes more than 55 pounds (25 kg) of pasta a year and about half a pound (0.23 kg) of bread a day.

👍 The Italian soccer team is known as the Azzurri, the word for light blue, after the color of their uniform.

👍 The official state motto is "Italy is a democratic republic, founded on labor" a statement that originates from Roman times.

👍 Italy is well known for its high fashion, and Milan is considered to be the fashion capital of the world.

Meet the family

Now you can start learning some Italian. The Rossi family will introduce you to different situations.

Benvenuto in Italia!
Behn-vay-noo-toh een Ee-tah-lee-ah!
Welcome to Italy!

**Noi siamo il
Signore e la Signora Rossi.**
*Noh-ee see-ah-moh eel seen-yoh-reh
eh lah seen-yoh-rah Ross-see.*
We are Mr. and Mrs. Rossi.

Mi chiamo Clara.
Mee kee-ah-moh Klah-rah.
My name is Clara.

Ed io mi chiamo Marco.
Ayd ee-oh mee-kee-ah-moh Mahr-koh.
And my name is Marco.

Clara, Marco, and their parents always speak in Italian. Beneath the Italian words is a guide to help you to pronounce it correctly, and the English is underneath that.

In bocca al lupo! – the Italian words.
Een bock-kah ahl loo-poh! – how to say the Italian words.
Good luck! – what they mean in English.

13

They will tell you about life in Italy – at home, at school, traveling and having fun.

At school

Clara and Marco go to **la scuola elementare** (*lah-skoo-oh-lah eh-leh-men-tah-reh*) – primary school. It is for children between 6 and 11 years old. School begins at 8.30 A.M., or earlier in some regions.

School is **tempo pieno** (*tem-poh pee-eh-noh* (full-time) with four hours of lessons in the morning, **la mattina** (*lah maht-tee-nah*), and three hours in the afternoon, **il pomeriggio** (*eel poh-meh-ree-djoh*). Other children choose **modulo** (*moh-doo-loh*) with four hours of school every morning including Saturday, with most afternoons free. Clara and Marco have a playground break at 10.20 A.M. This is called **l'intervallo** (*leen-tehr-vahl-loh*).

il campo giochi
eel kahm-poh djoh-kee
playground

la ragazza
lah rah-gaht-sa
girl

la palla
lah pahl-lah
ball

il ragazzo
eel rah-gaht-so
boy

With **tempo pieno** there is an hour for lunch. Some children go home but Clara and Marco have lunch vouchers to eat in **la mensa** (*lah men-sah*) – the school lunchroom. After lunch they play in the playground.

Lessons are called **le lezioni** (*leh leh-tsee-oh-nee*), so if you say **ho una lezione** (*oh oon-ah leh-tsee-oh-neh*) it means "I have a class" or "I've got to go to a class."

In the **scuola elementare**, lessons finish by 4.30 P.M. and all children have to go home. Children can get the school bus to and from school, provided they have their parents' permission.

In the mornings some children go to school before 8.30 A.M. as their parents are already at work, so they finish off their homework, or draw, or play games.

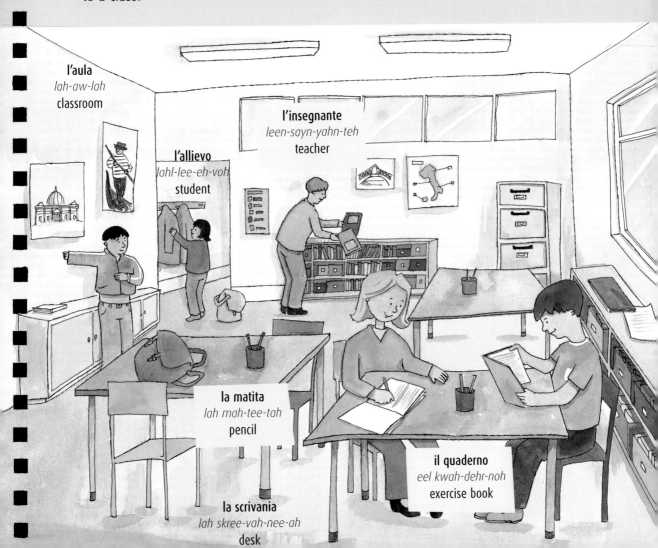

l'aula
lah-aw-lah
classroom

l'insegnante
leen-sayn-yahn-teh
teacher

l'allievo
lahl-lee-eh-voh
student

la matita
lah mah-tee-tah
pencil

il quaderno
eel kwah-dehr-noh
exercise book

la scrivania
lah skree-vah-nee-ah
desk

After school

Clara and Marco must do their homework when they get home from school. The amount of homework varies, with more at weekends. If they are given a project to do, they have a week to finish it.

Marco enjoys watching cartoons – **cartoni animati** (*kahr-toh-nee ah-nee-mah-tee*) on television, but Clara prefers reading. If they have time they sometimes play card games together. As well as playing volleyball, Clara goes to dance classes once a week and Marco goes to judo at the same time.

They are allowed to look up the Internet on the computer, called **il computer**, but only with parental supervision.

Sometimes Marco plays computer games or **i giochi informatici** (*ee joh-kee een-forr-mah-tee-chee*), while Clara prefers to read *Harry Potter* or *Lord of the Rings*. Italians normally have a large meal in the evening, even if both parents are at work during the day. Dinner – **la cena** (*lah chay-nah*) – is usually at 8 o'clock. Sometimes the television is switched on but they are too busy eating to watch it!

After dinner, it's time for Marco and Clara each to have a shower and go to bed. They both have to be up very early in the morning for school.

il computer
eel komp-yoo-tehr
computer

16

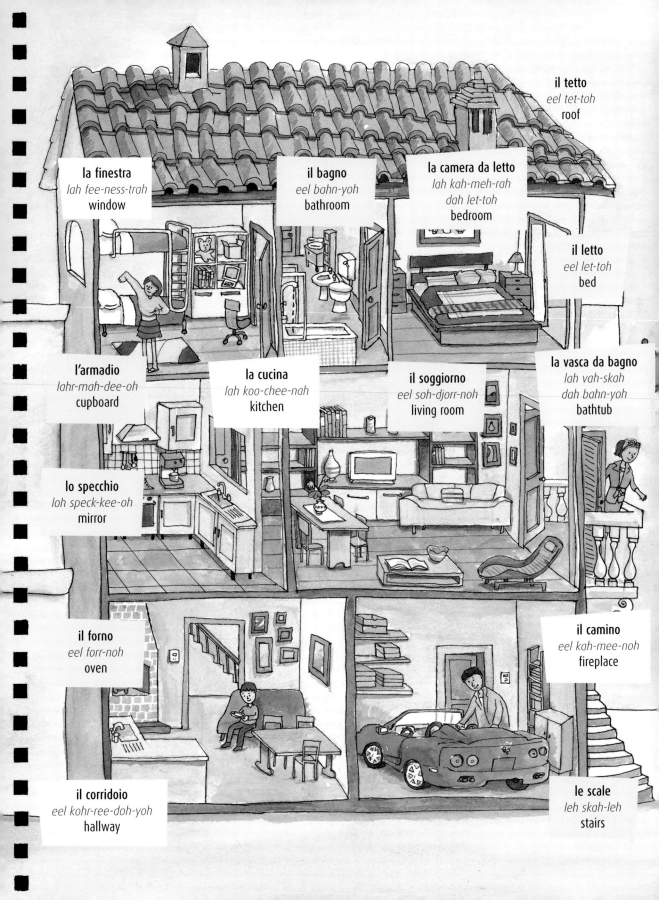

il tetto
eel tet-toh
roof

la finestra
lah fee-ness-trah
window

il bagno
eel bahn-yoh
bathroom

la camera da letto
lah kah-meh-rah dah let-toh
bedroom

il letto
eel let-toh
bed

l'armadio
lahr-mah-dee-oh
cupboard

la cucina
lah koo-chee-nah
kitchen

il soggiorno
eel soh-djorr-noh
living room

la vasca da bagno
lah vah-skah dah bahn-yoh
bathtub

lo specchio
loh speck-kee-oh
mirror

il forno
eel forr-noh
oven

il camino
eel kah-mee-noh
fireplace

il corridoio
eel kohr-ree-doh-yoh
hallway

le scale
leh skah-leh
stairs

In town

It's the weekend – **il weekend** or **il fine settimana** (*eel fee-neh set-tee-mah-nah*)! Everyone in the Rossi family is happy because there is no school or work. Saturday is market day and the whole family goes.

il comune
eel koh-moo-neh
town hall

la pasticceria
lah pah-steech-chay-ree-ah
bakery

l'ufficio postale
loof-fee-choh poss-tah-leh
post office

la statua
lah stah-too-ah
statue

il motorino
eel moh-toh-ree-noh
moped

la chiesa
lah kee-ay-sah
church

gli alimentari
lyee ah-lee-men-tah-ree
grocery store

la farmacia
lah fahr-mah-chee-ah
drugstore

il supermercato
eel soo-pehr-mehr-kah-toh
supermarket

il distributore
eel dee-stree-boo-toh-reh
gas station

In the afternoon Clara goes to the park to play volleyball (**la pallavolo** - *lah pahl-lah voh-loh*) with her friends. Marco goes in the car with his father to get gas at the gas station.

la macchina
lah mahk-kee-nah
car

Things people do

Italy has warm summers and cold winters in the north, but in the south, hot, dry summers and mild winters. The Alps have a mountain climate.

Many people have moved from the country to work in the cities and towns and only five percent of the population work in farming.

la pecora
lah pay-koh-rah
sheep

Italy is one of the world's leading producers of wine, olives, and olive oil. Other important crops are beets, wheat, potatoes, and rice, as well as corn, tomatoes, barley, rye, artichokes, and chili peppers.

Dairy farming is also very important (butter, milk, cream, and yogurt) and about 50 kinds of cheese such as gorgonzola, parmesan, and mozzarella are produced.

l'agricoltore
lah-gree-kohl-toh-reh
farmer

il formaggio
eel forr-mah-djoh
cheese

l'isola
lee-zoh-lah
island

l'uva
loo-vah
grapes

20

 Italy still has a very lively peasant-farming tradition.

Livestock include sheep, pigs, cattle, water buffalo (for mozzarella cheese), goats, horses (horsemeat is still eaten!), and chickens.

il bufalo
eel boo-fah-loh
buffalo

Il limone
eel lee-moh-nay
lemon

Italy produces a range of fruit such as melons, watermelons, apples, oranges, grapes, lemons, figs, peaches, nectarines, and nuts.

Fishing is another important industry, and for people living on islands, it is often the only source of income, apart from tourism. Mussels, shrimp, and prawns, sardines, trout, mullet, squid, tuna, and anchovies are all fished.

la barca da pesca
lah bahr-kah dah pess-kah
fishing boat

il pescatore
eel pess-kah-toh-reh
fisherman

21

Fish is very popular and is often served as an alternative to pizza in many restaurants.

la modella
lah moh-dell-lah
model

Italy's main exports include cars, machinery, vegetables and fruit, wine, chemicals, textiles, and some things for which Italy is world famous – clothing, shoes, and handbags. Many Italian men and women pride themselves on their appearance and often wear designer clothes such as Dolce & Gabbana or Prada. They change their wardrobes, including shoes and bags, so often that it is hard keeping up with them! They enjoy shopping at exclusive shops (there aren't very many clothing shop chains in Italy) and they are very proud of the "Made in Italy" label.

Tourism is a major industry and many Italians work in hotels and restaurants that are often family run.

il caffè
eel kahf-feh
café

la tavola
lah tah-voh-lah
table

il cameriere
eel kah-may-ree-ay-reh
waiter

Check out the Dolce & Gabbana and Prada web sites.

Things about Italy

part three

Did you know?

👍 The ceiling of the Sistine Chapel in the Vatican was painted by Michelangelo, who had to work while lying on his back for four years.

👍 The ruins of the Roman Forum, which was the center of government for the Roman Empire, are an amazing place to visit in the middle of Rome.

👍 Rome is home to the Colosseum, the arena in which professional fighters called gladiators fought sometimes to the death, for the entertainment of 50,000 Romans.

👍 The thermometer and the typewriter were both invented by Italians.

👍 The Leaning Tower of Pisa started to lean even before it was completed, as it was built on poor foundations.

👍 Italy has approximately 3,000 museums.

👍 Sicily is known for being home to the criminal organization called the Mafia.

👍 The first opera was sung in Florence about 400 years ago.

👍 Archimedes, the famous mathematician, was born in Sicily.

50 Italian history facts

1 **c. 9,000 B.C.** Etruscans settle in Italy. False teeth may have been invented by them – thay are known to have been in use from 700 B.C.!

2 **c. 8,000 B.C.** Greeks move to Sicily and southern Italy.

3 **Around 560–480 B.C.** Pythagoras develops his famous theory.

4 **510 B.C.** The Roman Republic is founded.

Ruins in the Roman forum

5 **218–217 B.C.** Hannibal's army, including elephants, marches on Rome across the Alps from Spain.

6 **49 B.C.** Julius Caesar becomes Dictator of Rome and is assassinated in 44 B.C.

7 **79 A.D.** Vesuvius erupts and destroys Pompeii and Herculaneum. Both are amazing places to visit nowadays.

8 **848–856** First medical school established in Salerno, near Naples.

9 **1094** The extraordinarily fine Basilica in Venice is completed.

Early anatomy

10 **1271** Marco Polo travels from Venice to China and brings back many new things – including ice cream!

11 **c. 1270** Eyeglasses are invented in Italy for those with poor eyesight. They are first used in Venice.

First eyeglasses

12 **1321** Dante writes one of the world's great masterpieces – *The Divine Comedy*.

13 **1436** The dome of Florence Cathedral, a great engineering feat, is finished.

Vesuvius and the ruins of Pompeii

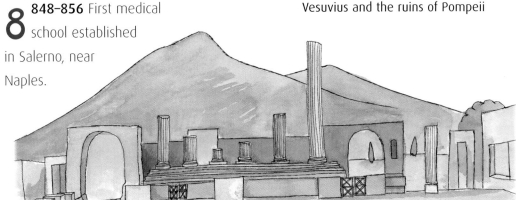

23

Can you find out when Vesuvius last erupted?

Explorers and sportsmen

Christopher Columbus (1451–1506) Most famous explorer of the New World – America.

Amerigo Vespucci (1454–1512) Explorer whose name was given to America. He was the first European to state that South America was a new continent and not part of Asia. The name "America" was gradually used for both parts of the continent.

Giovanni da Verrazano (1485–1528) Discoverer of New York (there is a bridge named after him).

Tazio Georgio Nuvolari (1892–1953) Outstanding racing driver of his era and winner of many races.

Tazio Nuvolari

Dino Zoff (b. 1942) One of the world's greatest goalkeepers who played 112 times for Italy. Also briefly manager of the national soccer team.

Gianfranco Zola (b. 1966) Played soccer for Chelsea FC (in England) and Italy.

Paolo Maldini (b. 1968) Soccer captain of AC Milan and Italy with record-breaking number of appearances for Italy.

Paolo Maldini

Sara Simeoni (b. 1953) High-jumper, 1980 Olympic champion.

Marco Pantani (1970–2004) Cyclist and winner of Tour de France in 1998. Died prematurely.

Francesco Totti (b. 1976) Captain of the soccer club Roma and plays for Italy. Has written a joke book which was a best-seller, with the proceeds going to charity. Since 2003 he has been a goodwill ambassador for UNICEF.

Francesco Totti

Look up Totti's web site **www.francescototti.com** to find out more.

Writers and philosophers

Dante Alighieri (1265–1321) Wrote *The Divine Comedy* in rhyming form.

Petrarch (1304–1374) Poet, scholar, and humanist who perfected sonnet form.

Giovanni Boccaccio (1313–1375) Wrote *The Decameron* – 100 tales in prose.

Niccolò Machiavelli (1469–1527) Political philosopher, his name now means cunning.

Niccolò Machiavelli

Alessandro Manzoni (1785–1873) Father of modern Italian novel with *The Betrothed*.

Gianluigi Bonelli (1908–2001) Creator of comic strip *Tex Willer*.

Dacia Maraini (b. 1936) Contemporary writer, feminist, and playwright born in Florence.

Artists and musicians

Giotto (c. 1267–1337) Most important Italian painter of the 14th century.

Leonardo da Vinci (1452–1519) Painter, sculptor, architect, engineer, and scientist.

Michelangelo (1475–1564) Renaissance sculptor, painter, and architect.

Raphael (1483–1520) Leading High Renaissance painter.

Titian (c. 1485–1576) Venetian painter, widely regarded as one of the forefathers of modern painting.

Michelangelo

Amedeo Modigliani (1884–1920) Painter and sculptor of the human figure.

Giorgio de Chirico (1888–1978) Painter who influenced the Surrealist movement.

Nicolò Paganini (1782–1840) Composer and violinist.

Gioacchino Rossini (1792–1868) His best-known work is probably *Il Barbiere di Siviglia* (The Barber of Seville).

Giuseppe Verdi (1813–1901) Composer of some of the world's greatest operas.

Gioacchino Rossini

Giacomo Puccini (1858–1924) Composer of *Madama Butterfly* first performed in 1904.

Arturo Toscanini (1867–1957) Conductor of classical music and opera admired by millions over a long career.

38 Debora Compagnoni is a World Ski Champion. She won two gold medals in the 1995 World Cup.

39 Lucio Battisti was a well-known Italian singer and songwriter, popular in the 60s and 70s. He composed hit songs for Italy's most famous female singers, Mina and Patty Pravo.

40 Giovanna Mezzogiorno won best actress award at the 2005 Venice Film Festival for her part in *La Bestia nel Cuore,* directed by Cristina Comencini.

41 Italians have won Nobel Prizes for Medicine, Peace, Physics, and Chemistry.

42 St. Francis of Assisi is the patron saint of Italy. His feast day is celebrated on October 4.

43 Italy is the fourth-biggest steel producer in Europe. There are stocks of petroleum, lignite, sulphur, and pyrites.

St Francis

44 Earthquakes hit southern Italy in 2002, killing 26 children.

45 Marco Polo's 13th century Asian journey lasted 24 years.

46 We know that pasta was introduced to Sicily by the Arabs when they conquered the island.

47 In 2004 Italians increased their pasta consumption to 3,500,00 pounds (1.6 million kilos).

48 In 1789 American President Jefferson designed his own macaroni machine.

Jefferson and his pasta machine

49 Pizza was invented in Naples in the 18th century.

50 Pizza Margherita (tomatoes, basil, and mozzarella) was named after the Italian queen in 1889. Pizza is made from flour, yeast, and water kneaded together. The risen dough is rolled into a circle and then topped with tomatoes and mozzarella and anything else you fancy. It is then baked in a very hot oven and takes only a few minutes to cook.

Making pizza

☞ **What is your favorite pizza topping?**

Let's learn Italian

*Join Clara and her brother
on vacation in Rome and learn
all about the capital city.*

part four

Did you know?

👍 The tomato first arrived in Italy in about 1550, from Peru. It is now an important ingredient in Italian cuisine, although it was thought to be poisonous until the 17th century.

👍 The only railroad that travels to the top of a volcano is on Mount Vesuvius and was built in 1880.

👍 There are more chocolatiers in Turin than in France and Belgium combined.

👍 Venice is built on 117 lagoons and has 177 canals.

👍 The Piedmont region of Italy is home to one of the rarest foods in the world, the white truffle.

👍 The American novelist, James Fenimore Cooper, wrote about Venice in his novel, *The Bravo*.

👍 The word for pasta comes from the Italian for paste, as the dough is made from a mix of flour and water.

👍 The Italians used forks 300 years before the rest of Europe.

👍 It is a superstition that unless you throw a coin into the Trevi Fountain in Rome, you will never return to the city.

👍 The famous film, *The Italian Job* starring Michael Caine and a fleet of Mini cars, was filmed in Turin. It was recently remade starring Mark Wahlberg.

Speaking Italian

When you arrive and hear Italian people speaking fast, you may feel frightened, but it's easier than you think to get started.

Like people everywhere, Italians are pleased when you make the effort to speak a few words of their language – just as you would be if someone speaking a foreign language came to your town but had already learned a few words of English. When they see you are trying, they will often smile and try to help you in return – especially outside the cities where they don't see as many tourists.

per favore
pehr fah-voh-reh
please

Start with a few simple words like "hello" or "good morning" and "good night."

Italians do not always say "please" or "thank you" but this is normal, not rude.

Then you can try **Va bene?** (*Vah beh-neh?*) with a rising voice to ask "Is that OK?" when you hand over some money for a postcard or some candy. If you want something in a shop you can point at it and say **Ha questo?** (*Ah kwess-toh?*) which means "Have you got one like that?"

buongiorno
boo-on jorr-noh
good morning

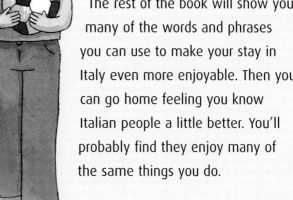

Hi! In the next few pages Clara and I will show you some useful words for your vacation in Italy.

grazie
grah-tsee-eh
thank you

buonanotte
boo-oh-nah not-teh
good night

The rest of the book will show you many of the words and phrases you can use to make your stay in Italy even more enjoyable. Then you can go home feeling you know Italian people a little better. You'll probably find they enjoy many of the same things you do.

39

Meeting people

Italians have different ways of greeting people they meet. They use polite greetings if they do not know the person well. With close friends and family they are less formal.

Sigor Rossi meets someone he does not know well.

Buongiorno, Signor Ferrari.
Boo-on-jor-noh, seen-yohrr Ferr-rah-rhee.
Good morning, Mr. Ferrari.

Come sta?
Koh-meh stah?
How are you?

Buongiorno, Signor Rossi.
Boo-on-jorr-noh, seen-yohrr Ross-see.
Good morning, Mr. Rossi.

Sto bene, grazie.
Stoh beh-neh, grah-tsee-eh.
I'm well, thank you.

Clara and Marco go shopping with their mother and meet some friends.

Ciao. Tutto bene, Marco?
Chah-oh. Toot-toh beh-neh, Mahr-kho?
Hello. Everything OK, Marco?

Bene, e tu?
Beh-neh, eh too?
Fine, thanks, and you?

A presto.
Ah press-toh.
See you soon.

Ciao, Clara.
Chah-oh, Klah-rah.
Bye, Clara.

40

Signor Rossi welcomes friends to his home for dinner.

Buonasera! Accommodatevi.
Boo-oh-nah seh-rah!
Ahk-koh-moh-dah-teh-vee.
Good evening! Please come in.

Buonanotte, Mamma.
Boo-oh-nah not-teh, mahm-mah.
Good night, Mommy.

Buonanotte, Clara.
Dormi bene.
Boo-oh-nah not-teh, Klah-rah.
Dorr-mee beh-neh.
Good night, Clara.
Sleep well.

Buongiorno is used to greet people during the daytime, and **buonasera** in the evenings. **Buonanotte** (good night) is used only last thing at night.

When people meet, they often like to discuss the weather.

Buongiorno, Signora.
Fa bel tempo oggi, vero?
Boo-on-jorr-noh, seen-yoh-rah.
Fah bell tem-poh oh-djee, veh-roh?
Good day, madam.
It's a lovely day, isn't it?

Si, fa molto caldo.
See, fah mol-toh kahl-doh.
Yes, it's very warm.

41

Making friends

The Rossi family has gone for a picnic by a river. After lunch, Clara and Marco run off to play soccer on the grass while their parents take a nap.

Ciao. Mi chiamo Pietro. Voi come vi chiamiate?
Chah-oh. Mee kee-ah-moh Pee-eh-troh.
Voh-ee koh-meh vee kee-ah-mah-teh?
Hello. My name is Peter. What are your names?

Ciao. Io sono Marco e mia sorella si chiama Clara.
Chah-oh. Ee-oh soh-noh Mahr-koh eh mee-ah soh-rell-lah see kee-ah-mah Klah-rah.
Hello. I am Marco and my sister is named Clara.

Ciao, Pietro. Quanti anni hai?
Chah-oh, Pee-eh-troh. Kwahn-tee ahn-nee ah-ee?
Hello, Peter. How old are you?

Ho dieci anni.
Oh dee-eh-chee ahn-nee.
I am ten.

Dove abiti, Pietro?
Doh-veh ah-bee-tee, Pee-eh-troh?
Where do you live, Peter?

Abito a Milano. Siamo qui in ferie.
Ah-bee-toh ah Mee-lah-noh.
See-ah-moh kwee een feh-ree-eh.
I live in Milan. We are on vacation here.

Pietro introduces his friend from the United States.

Ecco il mio amico Jack.
Abita negli Stati Uniti.
Ek-koh eel mee-oh ah-mee-koh Jack.
Ah-bee-tah nehl-yee Stah-tee Oon-ee-tee.
This is my friend Jack. He lives
in the United States.

Parli italiano, Jack?
Pahr-lee ee-tah-lee-ah-noh, Jack?
Do you speak Italian, Jack?

Mi dispiace,
non parlo italiano.
Mee dee-spee-ah-cheh,
nonn pahr-loh ee-tah-lee-ah-noh.
I'm sorry,
I can't speak Italian.

The rest of the family enjoys sitting in the sun.

la famiglia
lah fah-meel-yah
the family

il padre
eel pah-dreh
father

la nonna
lah non-nah
grandmother

la madre
lah mah-dreh
mother

il nonno
eel non-noh
grandfather

lo zio
loh tsee-oh
uncle

la zia
lah tsee-ah
aunt

Finding the way

Clara and Marco go to the nearby town with their new friends, Pietro and Jack. They look for the park while their parents go shopping.

Mi scusi, c'è un parco qui vicino?
Mee skoo-see, cheh oon pahr-koh kwee vee-chee-noh?
Excuse me, is there a park near here?

Si. Ce n'è uno non molto lontano da qua.
See. Chah neh oon-oh nonn moll-toh lon-tah-noh dah kwah.
Yes. It's not far from here.

Sempre dritto, poi all'angolo della seconda strada.
Sem-preh dreet-toh, poh-ee ahl-lahng-goh-loh dell-lah seh-kon-dah strah-dah.
Straight ahead, then at the corner of the second street.

Grazie.
Grah-tsee-eh.
Thank you.

Prego.
Preh-goh.
It's a pleasure.

Helpful words and phrases for asking the way

fra
frah
between

di fronte a
dee fron-teh ah
opposite

qui vicino
kwee vee-chee-noh
near here

44

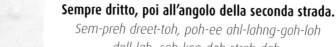 **fino a** *fee-noh ah* as far as • **a destra** *ah dess-trah* on the right • **dietro a** *dee-ay-troh ah* behind

On the way back to the square where their parents left them, the children get lost.

Ho sbagliato strada. Dov'è il parcheggio?
Oh sbahl-yah-toh strah-dah. Doh-veh eel pahr-keh-djee-oh?
I am lost. Where is the parking lot?

Il parcheggio si trova a destra, di fronte all'ospedale.
Eel pahr-keh-djee-oh see troh-vah ah dess-trah,
dee fron-teh ahl-loss-pay-dah-leh.
The parking lot is on the right, opposite the hospital.

Useful places to ask for

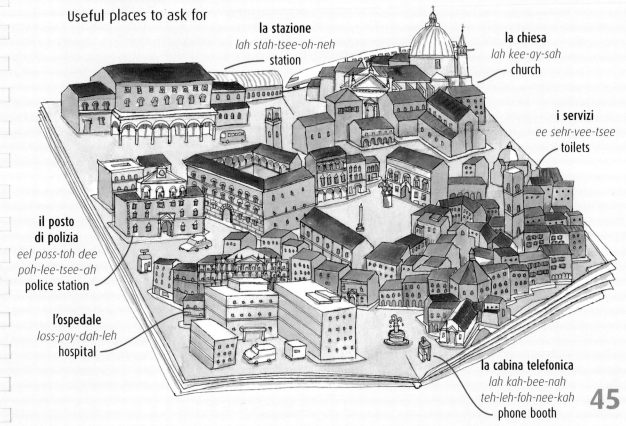

la stazione
lah stah-tsee-oh-neh
station

la chiesa
lah kee-ay-sah
church

i servizi
ee sehr-vee-tsee
toilets

**il posto
di polizia**
*eel poss-toh dee
poh-lee-tsee-ah*
police station

l'ospedale
loss-pay-dah-leh
hospital

la cabina telefonica
*lah kah-bee-nah
teh-leh-foh-nee-kah*
phone booth

45

davanti a *dah-vahn-tee ah* in front of • **a sinistra** *ah see-nees-trah* on the left • **di là** *dee lah* over there

Out and about in Rome

Rome, the capital, is 2,700 years old, and Italy's largest city.

il biglietto *eel beel-yet-toh* ticket ● il binario *eel bee-nah-ree-oh* platform ● l'orario *loh-rah-ree-oh* timetable

The Rossi family is at a café.

**Allora, un cafè, un thé,
una gazzosa e una coca-cola, per favore.**
*Ahl-loh-rah, oon kahf-feh, oon teh, oon-ah
gahd-soh-sah eh oon-ah koh-kah koh-lah, pehr
fah-voh-reh.*
OK, a coffee, a tea, a lemonade and
a Coca-Cola, please.

**D'accordo, signore.
Vuole un espresso o un cappuccino?**
*Dahk-kor-doh, seen-yoh-reh. Voo-oh-leh oon
ess-press-soh oh oon kahp-pooch-chee-noh?*
Certainly, sir. Do you want black coffee
or coffee with milk?

There isn't enough time for Clara and Marco to visit all the sights in Rome. Here are two of the places they could visit.

Refuge of the popes

Castel Sant' Angelo

Square with three fountains

Piazza Navona

49

Going shopping

Rome is a center of fashion in Italy, so Signora Rossi wants to look at dresses and shoes. Clara goes with her to a dress shop.

E' molto bello questo vestito.
Ay moll-toh bell-loh kwess-toh vess-tee-toh.
This dress is very pretty.

Vorrei provarlo.
Vorr-ray proh-vahr-loh.
I would like to try it on.

Certo, signora. Venga con me.
Chehr-toh, seen-yoh-rah. Vehng-gah kon-meh.
Certainly, madam. Come this way.

Clara, Marco, and their father go to the newsstand on the corner.

Quanto costano le cartoline?
Kwahn-toh koh-stah-noh leh kahr-toh-lee-neh?
How much are the postcards?

E queste due tavolette di cioccolato?
Eh kwess-teh doo-eh tah-voh-let-teh dee chock-koh-lah-toh?
And these two chocolate bars?

50

There are very good, lively markets in Rome and in most Italian towns and villages.
Here are some of the things you will see:

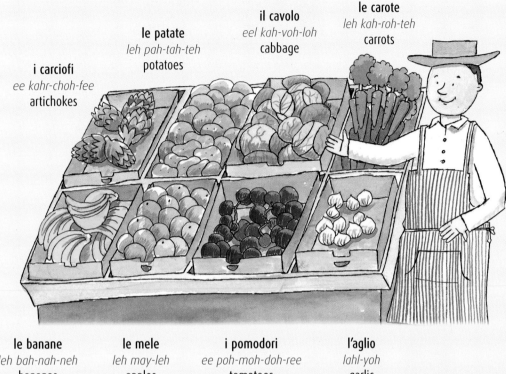

i carciofi
ee kahr-choh-fee
artichokes

le patate
leh pah-tah-teh
potatoes

il cavolo
eel kah-voh-loh
cabbage

le carote
leh kah-roh-teh
carrots

le banane
leh bah-nah-neh
bananas

le mele
leh may-leh
apples

i pomodori
ee poh-moh-doh-ree
tomatoes

l'aglio
lahl-yoh
garlic

Tre euro per il cioccolato.
Sessanta centesimi ogni cartolina.
Treh ay-oo-roh pehr eel chock-koh-lah-toh. Sess-sahn-tah chen-teh-zee-mee ohn-yee kahr-toh-lee-nah.
Three euros for the chocolate.
Each card is sixty cents.

Vorrei un giornale.
Vorr-ray oon jorr-nah-leh.
I would like a newspaper.

51

Eating out

The Rossi family goes for a meal in a restaurant. On the way, Clara mails her cards.

Vorrei quattro francobolli per spedire delle cartoline in Stati Uniti.
Vorr-ray kwaht-troh frahng-koh-boll-lee pehr speh-dee-reh dell-leh kahr-toh-lee-neh een Stah-tee Oon-ee-tee.
I would like four stamps for postcards to the United States.

Due euro e quaranta centesimi.
Doo-eh ay-oo-roh ay kwah-rahn-tah chen-teh-zee-mee.
That's two euros and 40 cents.

Now that Clara has mailed her cards, they can all go to the restaurant.

Avete posto per quattro persone?
Ah-veh-teh poss-toh pehr kwah-troh pehr-soh-neh?
Do you have a table for four people?

Sì, certo. Seguitemi.
See, chehr-toh. Seh-gwee-teh-mee.
Yes, of course. Follow me.

52

The family sits down and the waiter comes to take their order.

Siete pronti per ordinare?
See-eh-teh pron-tee pehr orr-dee-nah-reh?
May I take your order?

Si, siamo pronti.
See, see-ah-moh pron-tee.
Yes, we are ready.

Desidera qualcos'altro?
Deh-see-deh-rah kwahl-koh-sahl-troh?
Would you like anything else?

Buon appetito, signori.
Boo-on ahp-pay-tee-toh, seen-yoh-ree.
Enjoy your meal, sir and madam.

No grazie, basta così.
Noh grah-tsee-eh, bah-stah koh-see.
No thank you. That's enough.

53

A day out

The Rossi family is home again. Sig. Rossi is at work but the rest of the family is still on vacation. They go to the local tourist information center.

Le grotte sono aperte ogni giorno?
Leh grot-teh soh-noh ah-pehr-teh ohn-yee jorr-noh?
Are the caves open every day?

Si, signora, dalle dieci alle diciasette.
See, seen-yoh-rah, dahl-leh dee-eh-chee ahl-leh dee-chahs-set-teh.
Yes, madam, from 10 A.M. until 5 P.M.

Io preferisco visitare il castello.
Ee-oh preh-feh-rees-koh vee-zee-tah-reh eel kah-stell-loh.
I'd rather visit the castle.

No, mi piacerebbe andare al cinema a vedere Harry Potter.
Noh, mee pee-ah-cheh-reb-beh ahn-dah-reh ahl chee-neh-mah ah veh-deh-reh Harry Potter.
No, I'd like to go to the movies to see Harry Potter.

Andiamo al castello nel pomeriggio e al cinema questa sera.
Ahn-dee-ah-moh ahl kah-stell-loh nell poh-meh-ree-djoh eh ahl chee-neh-mah kwess-tah seh-rah.
Let's go to the castle this afternoon, and the movies this evening.

54

☞ **lo stadio** *loh stah-dee-oh* stadium • **le grotte** *leh grot-tay* caves • **il castello** *eel kah-stell-loh* castle

Quanto costano i biglietti? *Kwahn-toh coh-stah-noh ee beel-yet-tee?* **How much are the tickets?**

Summer school trip

Clara is going on a school trip to the Dolomite Mountains. She is very excited as her friend Alessia is going as well.

Buongiorno, Signorina. Ecco il permesso scritto dei miei genitori per il gruppo estivo.
Boo-on-jorr-noh, seen-yoh-ree-nah. Ek-koh eel pehr-mess-soh skreet-toh deh-ee mee-ay-ee jeh-nee-toh-ree pehr eel groop-poh ess-tee-voh.
Good morning, Miss. Here is the written consent from my parents for the summer group.

Ecco anche l'anticipo di 50 euro.
Ek-koh anhg-keh lahn-tee-chee-poh dee cheeng-kwahn-tah ay-oo-roh.
Here also is the deposit of 50 euros.

Grazie Clara. Lo segno qua che ho ricevuto il permesso e l'anticipo per la gita.
Grahtsee-eh Klah-rah. Loh sayn-yoh kwah keh oh ree-cheh-voo-toh eel pehr-mess-soh eh lahn-tee-chee-poh pehr lah jee-tah.
Thank you, Clara. I will write down that I have received permission and the deposit for the trip.

Quando dobbiamo pagare il resto?
Kwahn-doh dohb-bee-ah-moh pah-gah-reh eel ress-toh?
When do we have to pay the rest?

15 giorni prima della gita con un bonifico bancario.
Kween-dee-chee jorr-nee pree-mah dell-lah jee-tah kon oon boh-nee-fee-koh bahng-kah-ree-oh.
Two weeks before the trip by money order.

 Summer school trips are very popular with Italian children.

**Spero che ci sia ancora la neve.
Hai portato i tuoi stivali dopo sci?**
*Speh-roh keh chee see-ah anhg-koh-rah
lah neh-veh. Ah-ee porr-tah-toh ee
too-oh-ee stee-vah-lee doh-poh shee?*
I hope there will still be snow.
Have you got your snow boots?

**Certo, mi piace
molto camminare nella neve!**
*Chehr-toh, mee pee-ah-cheh moll-toh
kahm-mee-nah-reh nell-lah neh-veh!*
Oh yes, I love walking in the snow!

**Buonanotte, ragazze,
è ora di dormire.**
*Boo-oh-nah-not-teh, rah-gaht-seh,
eh oh-rah dee dorr-mee-reh.*
Good night, girls, time for bed.

O no, vogliamo leggere ancora!
*Oh noh, voll-yah-moh
leh-djeh-reh anhg-koh-rah!*
Oh, no, we want to read!

**No, Alessia, spegni
quella torcia e dormi.**
*Noh Ah-less-see-ah, spayn-yee
kwel-lah torr-chah eh dorr-mee.*
No, Alessia, turn off the
flashlight and go to sleep.

57

The scenery in the Dolomites is wonderful, both in summer and winter. ☞

A soccer game

Inter Milan and AC Milan are playing in a derby at the massive San Siro stadium in Milan. The stadium holds more than 80,000 people. Half the stadium is a mass of blue and black while the other half is red and black, with banners, flags, and flares.

Guarda, sta per fare un gol!
Gwahr-dah, stah pehr fah-reh oon goll!
Look, he's going for a goal!

Si, ha fatto un gol!
See, ah faht-toh oon goll!
Yes, he's scored!

58

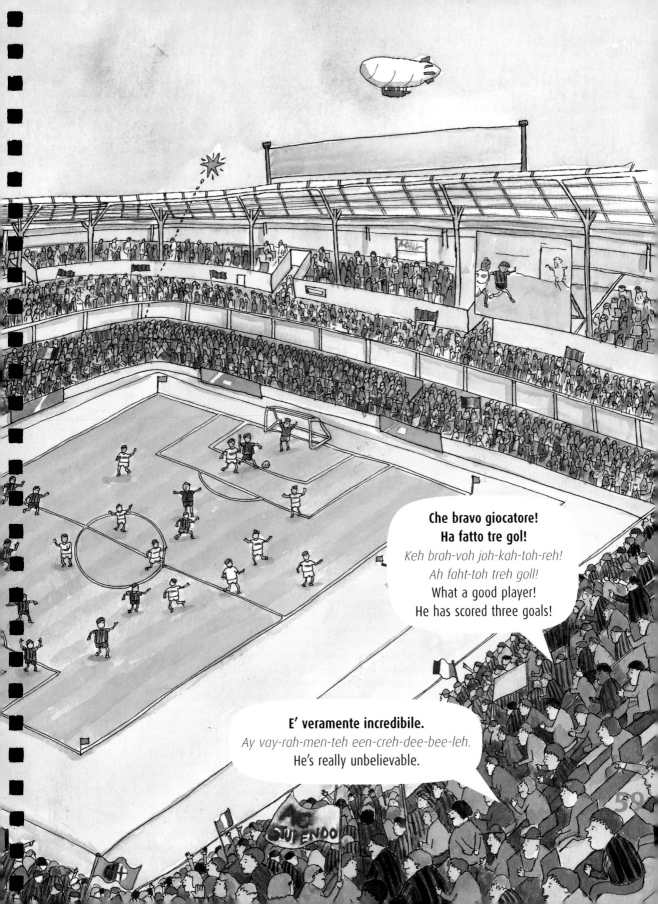

Illness and accidents

Italy has got an efficient health service. Some medicines and treatments are free, but others will cost a small amount.

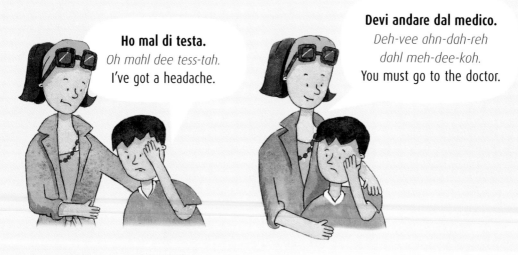

Ho mal di testa.
Oh mahl dee tess-tah.
I've got a headache.

Devi andare dal medico.
Deh-vee ahn-dah-reh dahl meh-dee-koh.
You must go to the doctor.

Here are a few little things that could go wrong.

Lei si è scottata al sole.
Lay see eh skot-tah-tah ahl soh-eh.
She has a sunburn.

Ho mal di schiena.
Oh mahl dee skee-eh-nah.
I have a backache.

Ha la febbre.
Ah lah feb-breh.
He has a temperature.

Bits of me

If you have an accident and need the doctor, it's useful to know the Italian words for parts of your body. And if you go shopping for clothes, here are the names of a few things you might want.

la testa
lah tess-tah
head

i capelli
ee kah-pell-lee
hair

le orecchie
leh oh-reck-kee-eh
ears

il collo
eel koll-loh
neck

i gomiti
ee goh-mee-tee
elbows

le mani
leh mah-nee
hands

le coscie
leh koh-shee-eh
thighs

le ginocchia
leh jee-noch-kee-ah
knees

le caviglie
leh kah-veel-yeh
ankles

gli occhi
lyee ock-kee
eyes

il naso
eel nah-soh
nose

la bocca
lah bock-kah
mouth

le spalle
leh spahl-leh
shoulders

le braccia
leh brahch-chah
arms

le dita
leh dee-tah
fingers

la pancia
lah pahn-chah
tummy

le gambe
leh gahm-beh
legs

i piedi
ee pee-eh-dee
feet

la maglia
lah mahl-yah
pullover, sweater

i blu-jeans
ee bloo-jeens
pair of jeans

le scarpe
leh skahr-peh
shoes

61

You can also say "golf" for sweater. ☞

Counting

1 **uno** *oon-oh*

2 **due** *doo-eh*

3 **tre** *treh*

4 **quattro** *kwaht-troh*

5 **cinque** *cheeng-kweh*

6 **sei** *say*

7 **sette** *set-teh*

8 **otto** *ot-toh*

9 **nove** *noh-veh*

10 **dieci** *dee-eh-chee*

11 **undici** *oon-dee-chee*

12 **dodici** *doh-dee-chee*

13 **tredici** *treh-dee-chee*

14 **quattordici** *kwaht-torr-dee-chee*

15 **quindici** *kween-dee-chee*

16 **sedici** *seh-dee-chee*

17 **diciassette** *dee-chahs-set-teh*

18 **diciotto** *dee-chot-toh*

19 **diciannove** *dee-chahn-noh-veh*

20 **venti** *ven-tee*

21 **ventuno** *ven-too-noh*

30 **trenta** *tren-tah*

1.000 mille • *meel-leh*

40 **quaranta** *kwah-rahn-tah*

50 **cinquanta** *cheen-kwahn-tah*

60 **sessanta** *sess-sahn-tah*

2.000 due mila • *doo-eh mee-lah*

70 **settanta** *set-than-tah*

80 **ottanta** *ot-than-tah*

90 **novanta** *noh-vahn-tah*

99 **novantanove** *noh-vahn-tah-noh-veh*

100 **cento** *chen-toh*

100.000 centomila • *chen-toh-mee-lah*

1.000.000 un milione • *oon mee-lee-oh-neh*

☞ **Even though the euro is the official currency, Italians still translate back into the old lire.**

Telling the time

Sono le tre e dieci.
*Soh-noh leh treh
eh dee-eh-chee.*
It's ten past three.

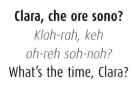

Clara, che ore sono?
*Klah-rah, keh
oh-reh soh-noh?*
What's the time, Clara?

Sono le nove.
Soh-noh leh noh-veh.
It's nine o'clock.

Sono le tre.
Soh-noh leh treh.
It's three o'clock.

Sono le tre e un quarto.
*Soh-noh leh treh
oon kwahr-toh.*
It's quarter past three.

Accidenti! Sono in ritardo!
*Ahch-chee-dehn-tee!
Soh-noh een re-tahr-doh!*
Oh dear! I'm late!

E' mezzanotte meno sei.
*Ay med-zah-not-teh
meh-noh say.*
It's six minutes to midnight.

Sono le tre e mezzo.
*Soh-noh leh treh
eh med-zoh.*
It's half past three.

Sono le tre meno un quarto.
*Soh-noh leh treh meh-
noh oon kwahr-toh.*
It's a quarter to three.

**Sono le tre meno
venticinque.**
*Soh-noh leh treh meh-noh
ven-tee-cheeng-kweh.*
It's twenty-five minutes
to three.

E' mezzogiorno.
Eh med-zoh-jorr-noh.
It's midday (noon).
or
E' mezzanotte.
Eh med-zah-not-teh.
It's midnight.

Italians normally use the 24-hour clock.

Days, months, and seasons

The Italians do not use capital letters to start the days of the week, months, or seasons.

gennaio *jen-nah-yoh* January	febbraio *feb-brah-yoh* February	marzo *mahrt-zoh* March	aprile *ah-pree-leh* April
maggio *mah-djoh* May	giugno *joon-yoh* June	luglio *lool-yoh* July	agosto *ah-goss-toh* August
settembre *set-tem-breh* September	ottobre *ot-toh-breh* October	novembre *noh-vem-breh* November	dicembre *dee-chem-breh* December

lunedì
loo-neh-dee
Monday

martedì
mahr-teh-dee
Tuesday

mercoledì
mehr-koh-leh-dee
Wednesday

giovedì
joh-veh-dee
Thursday

venerdì
veh-nehr-dee
Friday

sabato
sah-bah-toh
Saturday

domenica
doh-meh-nee-kah
Sunday

Acknowledgments

© Copyright 2006 by **Tony Potter Publishing Ltd.**, West Sussex, England First edition for the United States and Canada published in 2006 by **Barron's Educational Series, Inc.**

No part of this book may be reproduced in any form, by photostat, microfilm, xerography or any other means, or incorporated into any information retrieval system, electronic or mechanical, without the written permission of the copyright owner.

All inquiries should be addressed to:
Barron's Educational Series, Inc.
250 Wireless Boulevard
Hauppauge, NY 11788
http://www.barronseduc.com

Written by **Patricia Borlenghi**
Designed by **Trevor Cook** at HDA, Brighton and **Kevin Knight**
Illustrated by **Tim Hutchinson**
Edited by **Duncan Crosbie** and **Sheila Mortimer**
Language consultancy by **Fabiana Ramella**

ISBN-13: 978-0-7641-5954-1
ISBN-10: 0-7641-5954-2
Library of Congress Control Number 2005931815

Printed in China

9 8 7 6 5 4 3 2 1

☞ **Epifania** *Eh-pee-fah-nee-ah* (presents!) • **Natale** *Nah-tah-leh* Christmas